THE UNBEARABLE
WEIGHT OF MERCURY

by the same author

Unpacking Mr. Jones (Peterloo Poets, 1982)
From the Other Side of the Street (Peterloo Poets, 1985)
All-Clear (Peterloo Poets, 1990)

The Unbearable Weight of Mercury

JOHN LATHAM

PETERLOO POETS

First published in 1996
by Peterloo Poets
2 Kelly Gardens, Calstock, Cornwall PL18 9SA, U.K.

© 1996 by John Latham

A catalogue record for this book is available
from the British Library

ISBN 1-871471-63-X

Printed in Great Britain by
Latimer Trend & Company Ltd, Plymouth

ACKNOWLEDGEMENTS: are due to the editors of the following magazines: *Babel, Bound Spiral, Envoi,Frogmore Papers, Poetry Durham, Poetry Matters, Poetry Review, The Rialto, Smiths Knoll, Spokes, Staple.*

Thanks are also due to the editors of the following anthologies in which poems in this collection have appeared: 'Avalanche in Whitworth Park' in the *Lancaster LitFest Competition Anthology 1992*, 'Translation from the Latin' in the *Lancaster LitFest Competition Anthology 1993*, 'The Indelible Language of Trees' in the *Lancaster LitFest Competition Anthology 1994*, 'Conduct Unbecoming' in the *Lancaster LitFest Competition Anthology 1995* and 'Alligator Island' in the *Lancaster LitFest Competition Anthology 1996*.

The following poems in this collection have won first prize in national competitions:
'Not Walking on the Cracks', 'Great Roast at Nether
       Cholmondeley' — Aberystwyth, 1991
'Looking for the Wound to Fit the Scar' — Frogmore, 1993
'The Unbearable Weight of Mercury' — Aberystwyth, 1994;
       Charterhouse, 1994; Frogmore, 1994 and
       Hugh MacDiarmid, 1994
'The Bitter Taste of Wax' — Manchester,1994
'At the Deathbed of Desperate Dan' — Ilkley, 1995.

For Lauren Casalino, who saved me from drowning:
and with whom I travelled further than I knew.

Contents

The Unbearable Weight of Mercury

Quince, quina, quila, quiddity ..... A wax-bead topples
off the candle stick
limpets on his finger inching up the page.

His dictionary, lifetime's work, complete
except for this last entry that so troubles him
side-stepped years ago with: "Mercury. See quicksilver".
Now he can procrastinate no more: he thumbs his notes.

Extraction: Condensed out of vapours from roasting calomel
or cinnabar's vermilion crystals.
Healing agent: For boils and other pestilences
pour a goblet-full into a muslin bag,
immerse in boiling water
hold against the inflamed parts, ignoring all discomfiture.
Forecaster of wind and rain: Thirty gleaming inches
balancing the whole weight of the sky.
Signaller of agues and fevers: Sealed thread, sensitive
to heat or cold, placed snugly under tongue or in the rectum.
Conductor of the electric fluid: Metal shafts
dipped into pools of it, rotate smoothly without sparking.
Escapist: Tipped out of its jar, scampers table-tops,
leaps like lemmings, tight parabolas,
nestles between floorboards, inextricable.
Coquette: Dazzles all eyes, slips away from touch.
Source of pleasure: Romans filled deep baths with it
lay upon its sheen with wine or slaves.
Source of pain: Poisoned mirror — Narcissus first to die.
Warning on the dark-blue bottle: Be sure it does not drip
into cavities or lesions, especially of the face.
Note from Rebecca when she left me: I cannot kiss a man
whose mouth is a black graveyard.

Quetzal, quiblet, quicken ..... The candle splutters,
he dips his quill: "Quicksilver. See mercury".

Lightning Rod

Stormy days he'd stomp up Tryfan or Crib Goch — at the peak
upstretch his cane threaded with mercury, exhort its tip
to blossom in St Elmo's Fire, incite lightning to strike,
skelter down the silver, around the copper link,
plunge into the flask strapped to his belt.

He knew its power — to stamp glass serpents onto sands,
turn water into wine, innocents to prophets,
rip molecules to quicken our dead Earth. Rip Wilco, too,
fifty years ago. In sleep, it seemed,
head resting on the cairn, until fumbled unbuttoning
exposed a fern, livid, etched upon his chest.

To tame it he must understand, so every night by oil-light
in his garden shed, he galvanised gold-leaf and pith,
made sparks by rubbing rabbit fur on ebonite or amber,
turned the handle on his Wimshurst machine,
loading Leyden jars until they spat and crackled.

His grail, to come down from the ridge
with a flask of lilac water, boiling quietly,
feeding on trapped lightning, bleeding it away:
emasculated as Wilco who once could back-flip fences,
hop the playground on one hand, wouldn't cry
no matter how hard Shelley thrashed him: Wilco
who'd persuaded him to shed his calipers,
whose flesh he'd touched just once — cold, scalding.

Campers in the cwm said flickering violet light
showed him in staccato dance on Tryfan
— until a flash still burned onto their eyeballs
froze him, balanced on one hand.

Scent of ozone, suppurating fern,
shreds of blackened leather, gold tooth welded to his specs.

Under General Anaesthetic

Who am I I cry the dark
tide sweeping me away
I am me I'm here I call
but I can't hear me

stripped of everything
again I cry who am I
I am me I'm John
and so on and so on

the me I seek receding
speck of violet light
where am I where am I
I answer I am John .....

Looking for the Wound to Fit the Scar

A cool bright morning when noises travel best,
Wilco whooping on the hill.

Almost back, I ease my leg over the fence
drop into the field bull-dozed forty years ago

yet every tussock, hoofmark, stump,
leafless oak — the wisest in the world —
moss-slick gate into the upper meadow
crunch and taste of bluebell stalks
— all fresh as yesterday
and nowhere else, nor ever anymore.

Past the frogspawn pond to the forbidden corner
where lilac people drift around their gardens
seeing nothing, making me dissolve

and fears flood out: girls' voices, stagnant water,
German soldiers, the bog in Hobay Wood,
broken sparrows, undersides of logs
worms turned white with drowning
— and everything that clings and won't leave go.

Scar inflamed but still no blood.

Further back, outside the bathroom door
sent upstairs to comfort my small brother
frightened of the dark, I'm dry-mouthed,
too proud to shout my mother,
terrified of rustling in the attic roof
Hitler sneaking through the landing window,
blind tongue curling from behind. And yes, I'm bleeding.

Orange Gate

He painted my orange gate away. He, my father,
enfolded in whose jacket — sawdust, barley, ash —
I lost all fear of quicksands,
draughts that blew out candles,
cobwebs trailing in the night.

Painted black, the gate on which I'd always swung
peering through its slats at
big children off to school,
empty sleeves, splayed trousers
on the rag-and-bone man's cart
steam-roller that squashed Ann's cat
just sleeping, Mummy said,
though what, I wondered, were its dreams?
— and him, in overalls, sprinting back from work
to whirl me, draw me in,
toss me high and always catch me.

My orange gate, whose blaze in sudden sun
discolorations, crevices and blisters
I'd conjure up in bed
to calm my struggle against sleep's black yawn.

Hard, smooth; nothing to hold on to.

I scratched at it until I bled: no orange.
I scratched his face that night
when he bent to tuck me up.

Even now, as we huddle round his bed, swap stories
from fifty years ago, hoping their warmth
is seeping to him through his coma
russet, yellow, orange into black .....

Even now, I can't forgive him for painting out the gate.

The Sound of O

My bed high, cold. Striped pillow tastes of vinegar,
my new pyjamas have no memories.

Why did she serve me strawberries
in our willow-pattern bowl
the day the ambulance took me away?
It was their sweat gave me scarlet fever.

Each afternoon they take me to a tall, thin room,
I see her face, green felt hat
at the far end of a tunnel sealed by glass
that swallows my plea to take me home, my promise
not to write wicked words on the window-sill again
— that twists her mouthing, unfocuses her eyes.
I'm waving back but she can't see me.

The boy in the next bed has a cage over his legs.
Nurse whispers they're withered
with a wasting disease.
I dream them thin and dry under his sheet
until they snap like bracken.
When I ask him if he'll die
he says "I punish liars to doom",
won't look at me again
not even as they trolley him away.

Ten weeks. I no longer ache to touch her,
inhale her washday scent of suds and starch,
I ask Nurse Cora for bedtime stories now.

Not the violence of the wind
but the sound it makes, the o,
the o of isolation hospital, sorrow, polio,
the o her mouth made
when I spat at her through tempered glass.

Perhaps the Yellows or the Scent of Sun on Sand

Meandering high hedgerow lanes, from Criccieth beach
to Llanystumdwy, in sunlight, half a mile from home
I falter at a fork, try one way, turn back,
the other, scurry back. Air chills, darkens
as I scour the horizon, find no clues

and a stone solidifies deep inside my stomach
untouchable, weight pressing on my nerves

familiar stone over the last three decades
deposited each time I couldn't find you
you, or you — my cries so shrill, insistent
they drove you, you and you away.

But something in the evening light
flooding dry-walled fields,
perhaps the yellows or the scent of sand .....

and I'm a boy on the beach at Penmaenmawr,
I've lost my mother, I'm racing down the sand
flinging out my arms to every pale-limbed woman,
wheeling, screeching off when it's not she

taunted by the sea
dodging from right to left of me .....

Her arms are round me, I recognise the way.
The stone dissolves into a blaze of gorse.

The Lilac House

Curtains always drawn, door so long unopened
cobwebs draped its frame,
glistening in early morning sun.

They never ventured out into the lane
though once — peering through palings
from Mr Maddock's field —
I saw them ghost their garden, in lilac gowns
holding white enamel bowls.

I didn't ask my parents,
my frail image was enough — lilac ladies
reclining on chaise longues
with olives and lorgnettes,
pips discreetly stowed into lace handkerchiefs

or drifting lilac light in attics
searching for a lover who had never been.

Door yellow now, curtains wide,
Miss Bickerstaff wears ragged jeans
whistles out of tune. Last month, she waved
but I pretended not to see.
I will not walk that way again.

Instead, to reach the Post Office, on pension day,
I swarm up ivy on the warehouse wall
wriggle through the broken glass
drop down to Ditchfield's Alley
hurry past the worried house
whose weathercock is turned from me
whichever way the wind is blowing.

You ask why I'm telling you all this.
And all I can say is I thought you were lilac, too.

Making Space to Drape a Quilt

It is time to assemble a room for myself. A composite
of ones I've lived, shed skins and died in,
fevered ones I can't remember when I wake.

Its walls flawed glass, fragmenting birds and stars,
its entrance a tunnel on fern kneepads.
Greenness so profound that even in strong sun
the light is cool against my skin, my dreams.
Blemished wax to make my candles splutter, blaze,
lift out of dark, from fifty years ago, barley-sacks
we tied our prisoners inside before we hanged them.

I told the grown-ups I forgot her, went away,
but I stayed, sack twitching — broken bird — terrified
to touch, taste of pliant fingers in my mouth.

To drink, dew dripping from an iron stave,
scents of smouldering sage, lavender, mulled wine.
Hammock fashioned out of spider-web — in mist,
a longboat, drifting.

Hour-glass beating under fickle spirals of fine sand,
magic lantern pictures edged with hemp, drowned rainbows.

Often, when I wake, my hands are bleeding, cramped,
twists of hessian jammed into my nails
— and always, that yellow taste too sweet to bear.
It is time to assemble a room for myself,
ignite the fuse to block the tunnel's mouth
and when the hammock has stopped rocking
take this quilt, drape it quietly over the sacks.

Toucan

It has not been seen to move in years.

Hatched long before the birth
of anyone still living on this earth
it stands behind coarse netting
in Ibadan Zoo
its yellows and maroons subdued
sunk into its sinew

too old and sad to die.

Our eyes engage. I see an ocean
without islands,
an island without trees,
a tree stripped of all its green.

I'll show it true love
knows no boundaries,
trees thought dead may leaf again.

I stretch my arm between the mesh
feel its head relax
towards my palm's cradle.

Its neck-twist, strike
too sudden for my sight
I'm sucking blood out of my wrist
and cursing.

Eye still fixed on me
it hasn't moved

but I'm not fooled
— for a moment, we broke through.

Curtain Call in the Infirmary

The cast glides gravely round the ward.
In order of appearance; surgeon, registrar,
anaesthetist, housemen, nurses,
their timing, use of silences sublime.

Yet we, bedfast, are the principals
centre-stage, still-point of each drama,
one performance only, live theatre.
We've no scripts, auditions, understudies,
no prompter as we extemporise.
We keep our distances, like all great actors,
but each time one of us is wheeled away
we raise our hands in limp salute:
and when, unconscious, he slides back in again
we clap silently, underneath our sheets
— or fret if someone's absence grows
grieve as his things are cleared away.

Some mute or garrulous with stage-fright,
others drained by their performances,
we are a motley crew, random as a casualty list.

Voice withered thinner than a whisper
Tom communicates by eyebrow, shoulder-shrug.
Albert dozes in the wings
waiting for strength that will not come.
On-stage tomorrow, dissolving skull
to be offered to the surgeon's saw,
Joe glances in his mirror, pats his hair.

We'll have no memories of our performances
except, perhaps, in deepest sleep
characters will speak in tongues
and love-scenes will be played again
— the laying on of hands.

At the Death-Bed of Desperate Dan

Fingers graze and fidget in his face's stubble-field.

Difficult to credit, this beached whale in the bed,
gravel in his windpipe, engine almost failed,
once — a single mighty breath —
blew a stricken liner from New York to Liverpool.

Never desperate, easy to outfox, unbeliever
in Man's duplicity, he won through always,
bullets bouncing off his chest
swatting them away: "Durn them pesky flies".

Sunless granite, this unwrinkled forehead,
massive chin scoured daily with a blowlamp's flame,
buttoned belly ample with his aunt's cow pie.

His good deeds legion, prodigious, botched —
he carried his friend's cabin through a tottering mile
careful as a blindfold tight-rope walker,
sighed onto his knees, lowered it gently into place,
sneezed it into smithereens.

Life became too subtle for this legend
as he lumbered narrow streets
frowning at screen-flicker
wondering why folk ignored his outstretched hand
— emasculated by electrons, plastic, laser guns.

He lies in coma, skull pierced by the spear
he hurled into a cloud to puncture drought.
It had circuited the world when it struck him
from behind, gazing proudly into rain.

Dawn-light glints off a frozen mountain-top,
pines across the northern face still growing.

Rugbeians Killed in the Great War

Most are hyphened, with more forenames
than weeks survived in France.
For each, a full-face photograph
— boy-soldier, resolute
in brand-new uniform —
two pages on his school career,
boundless promise, leap to glory:

> **while charging at the head**
> **known as Toby to his men**
> **recapturing the flag**
> **valour, gallantry**
> **of grievous wounds**
> **of injuries sustained**
> **mortally, missing, lost**

Out of fifty, two exceptions.

Rupert Brooke, the golden boy,
two photographs
five-page eulogy:

Purcell-FitzDavies, T.W.B.C.
almost eighteen, dead
after four days in Flanders.

Photo smaller than the others
yet large enough to show
terror welling in his eyes.
His sentence glowered
from the page's emptiness:

> **fought as bravely**
> **as anyone who knew him well**
> **would have expected.**

The Great Roast at Nether Cholmondeley

All day, a feast of preparation. We scrub, slit, scour,
hone our knives, flay the beast — a roan. Rub garlic
on its every part, pound a willow stake into its heart,
its roundness on the groaning pole, a velvet pillow.
Sweat polishes the flame-lit skin of haltered Zachary
who turns the spit, gasps ash as each crack of the lash
burns away his punishment, warns him not to falter.
Each stealthy tear it weeps onto the sleeping flames
provokes a sigh, a leaping spear of green. High above,
in bustling ruby-light, a great oak's petticoats rustle.
We baste the beast with tallow caught in trumpets, pans
and horns. Wasting none, we store the rest for candles,
soap, sore throats. Ointment for torn strumpets, cloaks
against the cold. Waxen histories, for when we're old,
of springtime flowers, lips that shaped our singing.
Crackles, spitting, sobs of logs. Air diced by shadows
spiced with sage. Heat-whorls curling trunks of trees.
A ring of children — hunger-shackled, fringed by flame.
Its rib-cage for a cradle, ears for incubating eggs,
bones for scoops and ladles, hoop-whips, pegs. Hooves
for buckles, buttons — hair for twine. Hide, to keep
our suckling mothers warm at night — in lieu of wine.

Our goblets empty, stomachs full, wantonness abounds.
Seed is spilled with sighs and ancient sounds. No crime
to spread our supple thighs below the Milky Way: couple,
dream, caress in grasses sweet as hay — our silky bed.
Its silhouette grows noble as it thins. We give voice
to our sins, kneel in the church of its safe-keeping,
reel as flame-tongues flicker, lick an unborn foal.
Zack lurches to his wife, breathes to her the story
of how a dead beast wept for its lost glory. At last,
knife sheathed, he rejoices at her belly's swelling.
A kettle seethes. Our heads an arc of smudges, mouths
gashes in the dark. Embers redden, blanch. Ash settles.

The Painted Lady

That woman in the gutter, Sir, she's the painted lady,
mother of the hairless dwarf, the nun with testicles.
In other incarnations — for she surely is a phoenix —
she's been a goat, a fallen angel, a butterfly in milk.

Aged ten, 'The Nymph of Sorrow' lay naked on a mattress,
customers bought feathers to tease her as they chose.
If she giggled they won prizes and later she was beaten.
Stroke her, Sir, but gently. She'll be smiling inwardly.

She's lying in the gutter because she saw a snail, Sir,
someone's shoe closed over it and crushed its carapace.
No aspersions cast, but if you'd only walk barefooted,
snails might live, she would suck your toes in gratitude.

Some would say she's ugly — scarred face, purple goitre —
and yet her breasts have incubated hosts of orphan eggs:
not-to-mention rabbits, Sir. I have lain my head there,
dreamed of oceans, tar-smells, comforts of warm straw.

She's suckled, weaned me, caressed my festered sockets.
Now paint clogs up her pores, fatigue fogs up her mind.
Kick her if you must, Sir, her flesh absorbs all pain.
When you've finished, cover her. She has great modesty.

She had to swallow mice, bestride the greasy pole, Sir,
lick the strongman's lollipop, tend the secret grove.
Man-eating narcissus, siren, Theban feast — yet still
she stroked the hunchback's hump, bathed my empty eyes.

Kiss her if you will, she has great need of lips, Sir,
and mine are so familiar they can't engage her blood.
I've leeched her heat with acetone, jellyfish and plums.
Your moisture would refresh her. On her forehead, please.

She's singing, can you hear? Her voice is very low, Sir,
a lullaby to soothe the snail dissolving in her mouth.
She used to swallow adders, coals, lusts of drunken men,
but molten lead from crucibles trickled down her throat.

In June, they built a cannon to fire our painted lady,
fixed an arc of barbs, Sir, to make her loop and spin,
laced the oil with phosphorus. So emerald her diving!
The scratches were not mortal, the blisters only small.

Do you like it in the gutter beside my painted lady?
Fag-ash, dog-turds, tainted meat, sodden photographs.
Nuzzle in her manger, find your mother in her armpits,
whisper her a story, Sir, to keep her warm all night.

Not Walking on the Cracks

Old man keeps trotting past me, talking to himself,
finger sometimes stretching out, as if to test the wind.
    Forgive me praying for her thighs, Oh Lord,
    but I miss her, skin so supple, fine.
  here's another pavement-crack tread on it left-footed
  i know you won't forgive me unless i'm squinting blue
He skips, whirls, staggers, jogs knee-high capers,
head twirling to his music. I wonder if he'll fall.
  a leaf thank god it's autumn beech weather turning chill
    Between silk sheets, Lord, so good it terrified.
  bed-frame brass no wood goddam reach out for a chair-leg
  she asked what i was doing o my love i've got the cramp
  could be dangerous she said it was not a time for joking
Ballet-dancing now, bare feet, throat supplicating.
He's fisting tears. Come Sir, can I help?
    Next time, Lord, I hid a pencil in my pillow,
    forced my finger into it, to hold our ecstasy,
    but it pierced me, shrieking, dam-burst.
  she said you haven't surely and i said no love i haven't
  she said so why've you shrunk then turned the other way
    Give me another chance, Lord, to resurrect that day,
    I'll wear a willow bracelet, suck it furtively.
  skip across the hairline crack a second time for luck
  swat this fly i love it so its buzzing scares me sorry
I didn't see him tumble, he's lying on the pavement,
fingers curled in front of him, as if he's offering flowers.
    Smell of freckles, meadows. I need to touch a tree.
  not a lack of reverence i'll want your breast in time lord
  but you don't smell of sweat or taste of blood sweet tongue
    I stroke this sycamore, tap it sixteen times, Lord,
    we drift into our dance, our secret jiggety.
  i map your shoulders nuzzle gold hairs on your neck lord
  if you see a chicken hide if it finds you scratch it twice
He's crawling down the kerb-stones, talking to himself.
At times he halts, then lunges — as if leaping a ravine.

The Weight of Feathers

(for Alicia)

She is looking the wrong way. She is always
looking the wrong way.

She preens her feathers without stirring them.
She is about to lay an egg.

A light dazzles, shoals of daggers
in her eyes. She can't blink them away.
Her lids lower a curtain, pin-pricks slither
to the further side of scarlet,
soreness on the edge of memory.

The egg recovers on a cushion of straw.
She rests on it without weight,
moulds her body to the shape.

Fingers flick her to the side, pluck her egg,
rotate it — tap, tap, tap it on the fender,
rapping insistent as some old percussion,
clinical, not full of hope.
She wills herself towards it
but her wings are nailed flat to the floor.

Heavy feet approach, too slowly
for the rescue she's learned not to expect.

She stretches out across her history
the gap she'll never bridge,
gathers in the yellow threads
that ooze, thin, drip towards the rug

enfolds them in her feathers, cradles shadows,
fills with a song known only to the dumb.

Avalanche in Whitworth Park

The man rising from a bench behind the fountain,
lurching off the pavement onto new-mown grass
is wearing skis.

They leave contrails of flattened buttercups
as he circles a dalmatian, children with a kite,
rhythm perfect.

I want to ask him why, but his upturned eyes,
empty bottles underneath his bench, show me
he's at altitude

the Alps perhaps, a track through sunlit pines,
recent fall of powder-snow blanketing all sound,
in purest air.

Sacrilege to interrupt his journey, I turn away
but he calls me, flags me down, lifts his ski-pole
prods my chest.

His breath stale as an unventilated cellar:
"If you stare at people on slopes as steep as this
you'll start an avalanche."

The Aromatic Road to California

(for Sam and Sorrel)

Two-year-old child, nine-month-old dog
alone in a sixteen-year-old Datsun.

He drives fast, tongue-tip slipping
through his mouth's tight curves
mountains rear and wobble
as she licks his neck
sniffs his trousers' plumpness.

Chipmunks skid round tree-roots
wheels scorch a helix climbing Mummy
a sock under the floor-mat tastes of cupboards,
the mirror paints a future in a cloudless eye.

Pedals groan, plunge into a canyon
ocean opens to a sleek amphibian
gobbling the afternoon
as sunlight swerves through dust-motes
sucks an old meal out of leather.

Neither child nor dog will remember this journey
nor ever will forget it

and after the dog becomes a heap of bones
in a long garden,
the child a querulous old man,
sun-dried shadows flecking pine-needles
softening a corner
may flare in certain shades of light
subside into the earth — unseen

except by a child and a young dog
asleep in a sixteen-year-old Datsun.

Limitless

(for Tim)

"How much sky is there
in the whole world?"

I could answer that,
give the atmospheric mass
number of its molecules,
the global area,
rate at which air thins
outwards to the sun.

But as I look into his eyes
huge, open to the sky,
galactic deep
reaching far beyond the sun
I shake my head
tell him I don't know.

Conjuring Trick

(for Maunagh)

Pawnee, Pike's Peak, Sawtooth, Audubon.
He knows they're standing proud
behind this cloak that teases, swirls,
curls between the powerlines,
cabins of Gold Hill,
today a ghost-town once again.

But why should she — arriving
from the plains — believe it?
All she knows is illusion:
dog-howls drowning somewhere,
wood-smoke without fire,
patch of sky suggesting sun
and slowly quenching it.
Drizzle denies all clocks.

At last, it lifts,
they stand in blazing light,
he sweeps his arm towards them,
front range of the Divide:
Pawnee, Pike's Peak, Sawtooth, Audubon.

She shrugs, asks if they are relevant.

Obtuse Angle

I skip, take two long strides
at grazing incidence,
grasp the cemetery fence's
cool steel rail
— and leaning back
as Mr Pickering
once taught us
leap, double-kicking
high over my head:
my first oblique back-vault
for half a century
— and I am sailing.

But oh my spine on landing.

Biting back the pain
I spin round to my young friend
open my hands.

"You fool", she says.

We sit on a tombstone
eat stern sandwiches,
I wish moss
had cushioned granite
covering Jane Mugford
regretted wife of Thos.

But oh how I was flying.

And if he weren't already
in his own graveyard
how old Picko would have clapped.

The Bitter Taste of Wax

The cow is usually brown-and-white, full-uddered.
Often, in the long year since you ditched me
I've smuggled her into your house
she's stood at your piano, chewing Schubert
or slept behind the sofa you and I once sat on
sipped whisky, sensed exploratory signals
— and as your oboe soared she's lowed in harmony
I've grinned to see you frown and falter.
Pitchforked sheaf of hay to coax her up the stairs
she's sunk into your bath, sucking on the sponge
I used to soap you with on Friday nights.
Or, muffle-hooved, beside the bed
her breathing has ruffled yours and his
you've strained the dark for dreams slipping away.

Tonight, her warm tongue slithers
his shoulder-blades, his restless throat,
deposits a swamp in his left ear. He thrills
to its evaporative chill. Starless night
he can't see her silhouette
but he feels the perfumed promise of its weight.
Stiffened by the succulence of love-play sounds
— a viscous trickle, rather like mild chomping —
he leans to you, tongue furled
feather-skates the contours of your ear
whose wax's bitter taste I know so well
and as you twitch, murmur
his toes curl, he nibbles on your lobe:
"Piss off", you hiss; "It's half-past bloody two."

Underneath the mattress
I'm damp with tears from strangled laughter
but as your fingers drift to him
my stomach knots, I swallow feathers, swat away
affectionate slow strokes of Belle's tail across my face.

32

Birth-Day at the Great Sand Dunes National Monument

(for Lauren)

You, my lover, who thirty years ago today
lay pinioned inside your birth-canal

and since then have travelled light
slept often under stars, lived only
in houses with high ceilings, open views,
moved out whenever door-hinges grew stiff

you are lying pinioned beneath our comforter
oblivious of dunes
which fill the doorway of our tent
breasts, thighs, bellies,
recumbent in pink light

oblivious of me, my stretching out to you,
your spine a comma, arched away,
urgent for release.

And I, knowing all this, not knowing it at all,
impelled,

swing over, envelop you
breathe with you until our lungs are one,
ease your knees down from your chin
straighten out your limbs,
cup your head, turn it to the pulsing ruby light,
the sleeping sand

watch you stir, blink open, stretch up to me.

But I'm suddenly afraid, can't read your smile
tell if you'll push me away or pull me down to you.

Pelican

It surfaces again, rides up on a thermal,
glides, one lazy flap,
above our wave-lapped rocks
wheels, spirals in — hovers
covering the ocean

plummets, stretched, beak a scimitar,
rips into the water.
You wince, I shiver.

Repeat performances throughout the evening
as the back-drop deepens
from white-flecked blue
through yellow, orange, purple.

Plunging still
as we splash through moonlight
to our tent.

You lie open as the ocean,
I hover above.
Faint, sieved by our mosquito net
I hear wind rushing over feathers.
I tense for the concussion,
hesitate, as I imagine
the water's cumulative bruise.

We stroll midnight,
sand sifted by our toes.
High above, a speck drifts black
— and fathoms down
its shadow falters, surges for the sky.

Succubus

I am cauterising my blood.

I strike match after match
thrust each glowing tip
into the sac, swelling,
pendant from my chest.
Heat sears me
but still it won't leave go.

All day it has gorged on me
its crimson deepening.

I am its feeding ground.
It is leaching me away.

Match after match
until a phut of steam,
it curls, rolls off
into my stomach hair.

I flick it to the floor
stamp stamp stamp it
into my memory

of things that cling
drink me dry — and will not die.

Two Men and a Half

Please Mr Benson, I'm stuck on question number 4,
the one about two men and a half.

Five men taking six days is what you said,
so *two men* by themselves would take fifteen,
that's easy; or *three men* would take ten,
if weekends aren't included
and there's nothing heavy they've to lift.
But two and a half men puzzle me.

Is the half man dead, Sir? If so, it's really two men
so the answer's fifteen, just like before:
unless the men are put off by the body,
especially in warm weather. Was it summer, Mr Benson,
were they working in the shade?

If he's alive — I hope he is, Sir —
we need to know which parts of him are missing.

If he's got one arm, one leg, it's easy,
he'll do just half what they do,
the job will be finished in twelve days:
though that's only true, now I think of it
if it *needs* one arm, one leg, like picking apples.

If he's a lift-man, one arm's as good as two,
though if he's got no arms at all he's useless;
unless he stands on his head,
presses buttons with his toes. Is he an acrobat, Sir?

This is a very hard sum. Give me a clue, Mr Benson.
Is he a dwarf? Does he have a head, please Sir?
Why are you worried about two men and a half?
Are you alright, Mr Benson?
Are you going to have an accident, Sir?

Maloney's Contribution to Medical Science

It surely wasn't the whisky.

Anyone could slip, balanced on one foot
rearing out of green light
swirling midnight steam
above the slick enamel
of my high-sided Victorian bath.

And anyway, is a man not entitled
in his own house, frayed
by a day of mollification,
to take a half-bottle of Irish
a tape of "Das Lied von der Erde"
up the stairs,
rack the volume to the roof,
soak chin-deep, knees
pink atolls in a tropical lagoon?

Anyone could slip, not noticing
the soap bar on the floor
— and, rushed to Emergency
with such scarlet abdominal pains
could be forgiven, surely,
when quizzed by a doctor
deficient in solicitude
for not remembering the bottle

revealed a hobble-toed, limp-sore
fortnight later
by X-ray,
the word Jameson
in ghost-script, but wonderfully clear,
now reproduced on page 674
of the latest issue of *The Lancet*.

Conduct Unbecoming

I was the man inside the "Speak-your-Weight" machine,
Kings Cross Station, Platform 9.

I fulfilled all specifications: Thin, frugal
nimble-fingered in the dark,
not susceptible to cramp or diarrhoea,
accent neutral, voice well-modulated, strong,
mouth five feet two exactly from the ground
in stockinged feet. I enjoyed solitude and trains.

I seemed set fair for a spectacular career,
Platform 1 within a year or two; or even Euston.
Clients would re-route to hear me,
some made special trips with hampers, thermos flasks,
weighed themselves each hour.
Coins poured into me. My masters were well-pleased.

At the enquiry, many customers gave arguments
in mitigation: I'd never spared my voice,
I'd not told lies — except to those
who'd fed me foreign currency, or thumped me
if burred pennies wedged my slot.

But they were right to fire me for conduct unbecoming
of a man in a "Speak-your-Weight" machine.

She was so beautiful, smiling at some secret
as she turned from the whole world to face me, her throat
so close I saw fine grasses ripple as she swallowed.

They said if I'd confined myself to that first whisper
they'd just have censured me. But they couldn't excuse
my bellowing "I love you", six times
through miles of tunnels on the Piccadilly Line.
I went back every Wednesday afternoon, for years.

Last Marmalade

My new friend chews slowly: "Great marmalade!"

If you'd heard her, you'd have plunged
into your pantry's jungle, returned
jar in each hand for her to take away,
said if she'd protested: "It wants to be ate up."

This last jar looks empty, though it sucks my spoon
and when I hold it to the window
my sycamore is blurred.
Enough coating the sides,
if I poured in boiling water
screwed the lid on tight and shook,
to make weak cordial. But
your voice drifts back: "Don't struggle, son.
Everythin' worth twopence 'as to end."

Potato cakes with sunken lakes of syrup,
fried bread stiff with fat
to stave off cold and diarrhoea,
pies, pickles, bottled gooseberries, damson jam,
rum-tipsy Christmas puddings
boiled for days in muslin bags
and stuffed with sixpences.

"Thes plenty where them came from
and more besides." There always was.

Your larder I mouth-watered in
for almost sixty years,
its shelves bare now but for this jar
whose bottom my spoon circles
scrapes up the final bead

which I spread, half on my toast, half on hers.

Alligator Island

"yerthani .... methithur .... stithrinth .... ALLIGATOR"

His tongue has slipped its 90-year-old halter
modulates a fog of sound from which odd words lurch out.
We flail to find his meaning, while he, hearing only
the clear-sky version, sits, wills us to enlightenment.
Alligator. We blunder swamplands,
plunder from the undergrowth handbags, aphrodisiacs,
worry-teeth, cold eyes, hazards of jungle dentistry.
He frowns, expounds again — and "GARLIC" flickers
on a rumbling sea, we guess alligator soup,
he spreads his hands, rejoicing.
We spin out its preparation, dodge his eye,
argue over basil, chives, its flesh's saltiness.
We let it simmer while he yawns
and when he glazes over, turn it off.

Agitated, he mumbles out of sleep
"yerthani .... methithur .... stithrinth .... ARCHIPELAGO"

I wonder if he's sailing, afraid of coral reef
or if again he's one of a family of islands,
as you were, Uncle, fifty years ago,
when I'd watch you dealing cards around our table,
or straight-bat blunting the opening attack
while I fulminated at your lack of violence.
But not today, as we bury your last sister,
you stand, bare-headed in lashing winter rain
crumble soil into a hole you cannot see
fingers drifting your palm's emptiness
— your archipelago has shrunk
to a stump of granite in a rising sea.

Words trundle out of Amen silence:
"yerthani .... methithur .... stithrinth .... APOTHEOSIS"

Closing Time

I've just tried to leave, but I can't close this door
you were always standing at, waving goodbye,
from the day you first let me go to school alone
to our last meal together, before the ambulance.

We've put it on the market, one year to the day.
Geoff's painted it throughout, re-washered the tap
whose years of stealthy drips
ploughed an olive furrow in the bath,
replaced your cooker's wonky thermostat:
"Saves electricity, my pies cook quicker",
cemented the cracked driveway, re-set
slipped slates on the roof — all those jobs
you said we shouldn't fuss about.

We've cleaned out everything, mostly to the tip,
though we gave your clothes to Oxfam, his too,
except your shoes, misshapen by those bunions
you tried to hide from everyone.

Those gifts, rewrapped in the spare wardrobe
— did you feel they were too posh for you?

We invited your grandkids to take anything
in memory. They all chose from your kitchen
— baking tray, pie dishes, chopping board,
rolling pin still veined with flour,
the brush you moistened pastry with
before you tamped it, carving knife so honed
its blade had turned convex
— except Meg, who picked his wellies
from the greenhouse
those you gardened in after he died. She said
they smell of you and Grandad jumbled up
she wears them each time she needs to worry.

We boxed your photos, to sort when we feel ready,
crinkled notes in pencil on brown paper scraps:
"Suet, lard, 2lbs of carrots". "Corsets".
"Pickling spices", "Broken biscuits", "Slugs",
"Smokey died peacefully at 2.20 pm, aged 17".
"John married today". "Geoff married today".
No mention of divorce.

When we scraped our knees
you didn't listen to our words, just our distress,
you'd scurry for the medicine box
dab TCP or iodine on our wounds,
and if it hurt: "That means it's getting better."
Well, mother, it hurts. This last year hurts so much
I must be getting better fast.

I'll tell my story as I wander rooms with you,
trawl silences in corners, long-gone cupboards.
It won't be seamless, complete or understood
— just strips of skin peeled from me
glass-shards crunched between my teeth
or pocking my bruised wrist with rainbows.

You for sixty years, she for only three.
You gave me everything you had. At the end
she rationed me until my hunger disappeared.
Yet I bleed for loss of her, not you.
I want to show you to each other,
lay you both to rest, so I can sleep.
I want to discover if your death-mask told the truth.

I can't succeed if I take prisoners. Not this woman
seeking out uncharted routes,
gooseflesh and a distant flute her only compass.
Not this little girl in ribbons, eighty years ago
who gazes from my bedroom wall
— and sometimes, when I'm struggling, my mirror.

I'm in the wrong room. This isn't you, silk-clad
in a pine box

ring-finger naked,
hands rigid in symmetrical repose,
lips a pencilled arc of disapproval
face genderless, forbidding all trespass.

No trace here of the woman who
ravaged in her death-bed three days ago
gave Ann her recipe for damson jam,
cradled Shane to soothe his teething.

This isn't you, in violet light.
Or if it is, Mother, why did you deceive us?

***

You're dead, cremated, signed off in the books,
I'm racing back to feel her arms around me
tell her how my trip was, start to cry.

Tail winds speed me to Chicago, I skin-teeth
an early plane, so as we glide above thin cloud
I lift the phone to ask her to set out for me, now.

I'll hear her voice in seconds. No answer,
she can't be out today. I try twice more
and fail, have to settle for the old plan.

Her arms warmer even than my memory. I lie waiting
for the silence that leads to passion, peace.
I don't need her overfull apology.

He'd squeeze my shoulder in the dark, I'd hypnotise
my younger brother not to wake, slide out of bed,

sit shivering, his heavy coat draped round me,
breathe its scents of paraffin, tobacco, straw,
while he made a pot of tea, raked sullen ash,
stacked kindling, blew faint orange into flame,
settled in his chair, me squatting at its foot.

He clicks the bakelite. The wireless chunters
into life, snorting as he spins the yellow knob.
Song-shards break into my head and zip away,
foreign words people wouldn't really speak
so who was tricking me, and why? Homing in
to excitements that crackle over oceans, now
in darkness, at the speed of light to Lupin Lane.

Madison Square Garden, New York, America, 1946
Joe Louis, Brown Bomber, Shufflin Joe
defends his long-held title against Billy Conn,
local boy, white hope, whose speed, they say,
will see him through. Baying, roars and grunts
fade in and out our living room, his knuckles
white against his cup, words like gumshield,
parry, southpaw, feint, weave magic tapestry,
I'm sticking up for Joe since his real surname
is Barrow, same as my mother's. We're family.

I want to rest my head against his overalls,
hold back because boys should not be sissies,
teeth chattering until Joe's uppercut blasts Conn
into that niche of my memory labelled : "once".

He'd click the sound away, pour us second cups,
fiercer, colder tea, light another "Capstan", tell me
the greatest was a Jack — same name as him — Dempsey,
the "Manassa Mauler". His voice shed decades
as Firpo, Carpentier were savaged: Tunney, too,
the night of the long count, but the ref was bribed.

Seventy years after Dempsey was cheated of his crown,
ten after my father died — never abroad, whole life
within a stone's throw of Rocksavage — driving desert
north of Santa Fe, I spot a sun-bleached sign: Manassa.

In my dream a small boy punches air, leaps sage, cacti,
mustard grass, kneels, rests his head against my knee.

***

Fridays set aside for her replenishment.
I leave early, come back late,
she has the cabin to stretch out in
meditate, practice tai chi.

No household chores or schedule
except an hour with her masseur
whose artful hands
smooth the week's jaggedness away.

That day, I'm home a little early,
she's standing in our bedroom
folding the green sheets
we'd slept and loved between last night.

Before I've time to greet her
she flushes, snaps at me:
"Don't look at me like that.
I do the laundry sometimes, you know."

The village illegitimate — four days old
when your mother wrenched away
to a new life across an ocean.

Schooled to curtsey to your betters
keep your inkwell clean
do always only what you were told,
you won, each week, a silver star,
fending off the goblin
they said could smell bad blood
and would gobble you
if you relaxed and were not good,
still terrified, eight decades on,
your kids might learn your shameful story.

No wonder it was hard to let us go
— dabbing ointment on our wounds,
tying bandages in bows, so we'd know
they'd be easy to take off,
kneeling at our bathside
shampooing, soaping limbs
as far into our teens as we'd allow.
Stroking your only man throughout his coma
your eyes drilling his blindness
willing him to live,
your fear, each time we pulled away
less for your new abandonment
as our stumbling in the dark you knew so well.

Now, you thank your friends for dropping in,
nurses for inserting needle, drip.
"Yes, I'm feeling better." "No, I'm not in pain."
"Sip of water please, if you get time."

You twist, cry out, but only in your sleep
when pain pulls ahead of morphine.
You're carrying your shame safely away.

Sore from last night's nibbling,
my body's stickiness
too sweet to shower away,
I slowly strip our bed
— cool, clean sheets
will stroke our skins tonight.

I shiver as I recollect
last night's spurt of flame
— clothes torn off
flung around the room —
incinerating worries
harboured these past weeks

ignition the moment
she raced in late from work
my hardening swifter
than my comprehension,
she already softened
when we touched.

I gather scattered garments,
sink my face into her shirt,
thrill at a twist of black
half-hidden by a shoe
— silk she'd tossed away
before she pulled me down.

I lift it with one finger
twirl it in the sun
blink at whiteness
blaring from the black,
unfold it, find a chain
of overlapping stains

she'd carried home
— chalkiness I know too well.

You're sitting to the coal fire, knitting.

He's leaning to the dartboard on the door,
arrow pinched between his thumb
and middle finger, point stabbing the air
until he's plotted the trajectory
to double-top.

He flicks his cufflinked wrist.
Feathers corkscrew
round a swift parabola,
the dart strikes wire, bounces back
flips over like a high-board diver,
sails higher than before,
above his upturned grimace
between the lampshades' chains
slows, glides down,
quivers once, as it sticks
perfectly upright, in your head.

You shiver, as if a breeze has washed you.

You nod to the rhythm of your needles
— so do the feathers.
You look like Pocahontas
in my story-book. I want to laugh
but he's ashen, sweating,
he mouths a prayer
as he sneaks behind your chair
closes trembling fingers
round the shaft, eases it out.

You feel his shadow, fidget,
smile up at him, knit on.

I smuggle it away, and in bed
inspect the steel for blood; feel disappointed.

I'll sow doubt
inside his eyes that gaze out
mocking mine,
rack him, make him singe
until he'll cringe
at every heart-beat,
blister his lush lips
until her fingertips
would weep to touch him.
I position him with care
sink into my chair
relax and watch him peel
as swelling heat
climbs up his feet
thighs, throat, the tree behind him.
His nerve-ends bleed
I long for him to plead
as flame-teeth nibble him away.
He'll soon have taken leave
and when she fails to find him
she will grieve.
Only his eyes remain
quizzical, forgiving
no trace of anger, pain.
They force mine shut
I double over
fires rampant in my gut.

I kneel, sift
cold ash through my fingers,
watch it fan and drift
away. I lower my face
into its shelter
ask to find the grace
at daybreak's rim
to close the album
wish her well with him.

Eight decades since these fingers
limp in mine, stretched out
into dazzling new light
failed to find a mother's skin
to learn the world by,
a father's curls to cling on to.

Fingers I've always known
the smell and feel of,
which steadied me on rocking-horse
and wind-lashed nights,
coaxed fevers from my forehead,
chafed back into mine
what Jack Frost had sucked away.

Fingers which, as milk clouded
the speckled hazel of your eyes,
your tongue's swelling
sponged out words,
fashioned a new language
to greet, ask, answer,
thank and say goodbye

— and last night
when a baby's name was spoken
rose out of day-long coma

inviting your great-grandchild
to play with you
a game we are all born with.

I pray you felt his fingers' tug
their clutch and grubbiness
before he wriggled off
and you sank back.

Cooling but still warm in mine.

Guitar-notes waft from somewhere in the Plaza. She
smiles in sleep, our dog a rumpled shadow
on the rug beside her bed.
I squint through swirling wine
at forsythia in moonlight, its yellow
a shade I've seen just once before —
on the postcard my father always treasured,
in pencil: "Feeling a bit better, now. Love, Mum".

Seven decades ago, he ten years old,
her seaside trip a month before she died
emptying the family's tin box
stowed up the chimney,
his jar of farthings, silver threepences;
their hope, salt-air would stem her wasting
thin the growing huskiness
that made her voice so sweet.

She murmurs in her dream, fostering my vision
that sage-brush-scented air,
peal of mission bells,
crimson soil of Sangre de Cristo Hills,
tumbleweed careering the horizon
— would reopen her to me
upturn her resolution to move out.

They knew Scarborough couldn't cure throat cancer
but it was worth their loss of savings
her frigid deckchair on the sands
to give Jack one last week as a child.

I hoped Santa Fe at least would give remission
but as a wisp of cirrus subdues the pallid light
she shivers out of sleep, blinks open, frowns at me.

All day we've watched you slowly drowning
your throat's commentary more voluble
with each protracted breath, and death
creeps two notches higher
slithers one notch back.
You're too far out to catch a lifeline,
all we can do is hold your hands.

      Deckchaired, in a floppy hat,
      you're wickets, signpost, guardian of my loot
      prisoner to bury in the sand.
      Waves spread, thin, skirt my barricade
      slip under drawbridges
      surround the castle walls.

Each time gurgling subsides, ooze, black,
viscous as molasses
dribbles from your mouth
trickles your chin.
Geoff, queasy stomach a family joke,
sponges it away
moistens your bruised face, pale forehead.

      Your hair a sunlit tent, face my cloudless sky
      you flick my string of beads
      jig my wooden rattle
      deftly draw out safety pins
      unwrap my sour towel
      stroke messiness away
      bathe, powder me until I kick the air.
      You suck my toes one by one, swallow them.

Chains of bubbles navigate your windpipe's flood
silences between them stretch — one thins away.

      Sundown, still water, child whispers.

She parts the velvet curtain
promenades in front of me
adjusts, smooths, spins,
looks over her shoulder
in the gilt-edged mirror
asks me if it hangs well
matches her complexion
if the length looks right
too much shows, too little.

I'm tipsy on the fragrance
of her hair spilling down
green silk. I swallow
at her throat's faint pulse
her nipples' mild assertion.
This dress for her new life,
her new apartment,
the space away from me
she says will do us good.

She swirls into the mirror
arches back. Moonlight,
wine, last year in Umbria,
she's dancing in bare feet,
we sweep across the moon
lie laughing, panting
in warm grass. I reach out
to her, but she stiffens
scowls and turns away.

Tins in every room: blacking, toothpaste, buttons,
stamp-hinges, biscuits, farthings,
dolly blue, Dubbin — my favourite smell —
but if **the tin** was mentioned
then like the hill, the field, the cave
in my bold compass of the world
it meant just one — on the middle shelf
of the built-in cupboard in the living room.

Shiny, battered, lidless, communal
— stuffed with maverick items
too useless to be sorted, too precious
to be slung, too many to remember,
too secret to let slip away. So
once a month perhaps, no-one else around,
I'd spread the Daily Herald on the table,
balance on the armchair's rim
slide the tin's great weight towards me
climb down, precisely as a spider,
totter parquet, stumble on the rug, tip it out.

Stubs of candles, sealing wax, gnawed pencils;
three pieces of shrapnel from the German bomb
that made a puny crater in Fletcher's field,
rusty washers, brass buttons tinged with green,
grommets, beeswax whose fragrance made me drowsy,
a lump of substance unknown to mankind,
ball of fluff-blurred plasticine
I'd squeeze until it softened;
thumb-tacks, safety-pins, an 1820 groat,
corrugated conkers hard as granite,
curled photo of a woman you said you didn't know.

Unchanged from year to year, yet always
something new, our family's history
preserved in its detritus — but now, forty years later,
though I scour the house all afternoon, it's gone.

I haul it in, spill them out over the deck,
kneel to them, savouring their smell.

I've netted the memories I'd expected,
they make me smile or bite my lip, guide me
down the paths of our old journeys.

But it's not we who walk these trails
but effigies of us
who don't stray, play tricks,
leap ferns to clutch a vine, or hide.

Those memories that move me most
are ones netted by her, not me.

And so I shiver when she tells me

that when finally I found
I could soothe our puppy's keening
his first night with us, with stories
I'd made up for my kids,
she stroked the shadow of my spine
as I was whispering to him;

and that when we strolled
Assisi's sacred woodland
found a silver medallion
covered by dead leaves
and put it back,
she thought this would be the place
for us to marry.

My deepest loss is not what might have been
if we'd continued,
but what you'll never show me now we've not.

Your spring only in old photos.
Three-year-old in laced-up boots
with empty basket, lip-biting
at the threshold of a giant room:
posed at a table with crayons,
picture-book, eyes troubled
by a black sheet's spindly legs
and missing head, raised finger
forbidding you to breathe.

Your summer, awakening my senses:
skin cool or toe-curl-warm
on mine; eyes a hazel blanket
softening the dark; your milk
the taste of sleep; breast-smell
straw; wash-day songs hovering
in steam. You pluck a shirt
out of the sodden pile, peg it
from your pinny's ample cache.

Your drift to autumn imperceptible;
crust-hands kneading, rolling dough
shaping promises you always kept,
kneeling to your oven, heaping
pies and scones into our arms,
playing games too old for words
with infants carried in by me,
and as your twilight stretched,
by them, on their wide shoulders.

No winter, just a sudden chill,
a breeze, a fluttering of leaves,
crisp, into an overflowing basket.

You avoided centre-stage. The spotlight caught you rarely:
when Miss Hutton called you forward, pinned a star
onto your blouse; the mornings Geoff and I were born;
and three times — in crib, taffeta and now pine box —
in this sandstone church you lived your life in sight of,
from whose battlemented shade I blink into the light,
turn away for six long months, from you, Mother, to her.

If she'd not been fleeing, swinging round from time to time
to slash me with her scythe; if I'd not been pursuing,
whirling my lassoo, wrenching hemp around her neck,
we might have noticed each other's slow bleeding,
dressed each other's wounds, shared a pillow once again.

But my head those months throbbed with crimson clutter
which at night turned into demons gobbling my sleep
— while she found sub-texts to all my smiling questions,
her nerves so raw even my shadow weighed her down.

Our bones, once-supple, creaked and calcified

while I, in secret, became a torturer, strangled her
with silk, hung him from an iron hook to drip away,
tied them naked back-to-back, smeared honey over them,
opened a casket pulsating with read ants: lay bloated
under rhubarb leaves, waiting for the gardener's blind fork.

Until that moment in a blizzard on a Coloradan pass
when I looked at her and did not want that railing fury,
looked into the mirror, closed my limpet eyes. At last
I had the courage to draw the veil, and when I told her

red smoke thinned, drifted away, our aubade began,
we stretched out, touched — no clutch or pressure —
sponged each other's skin until our pores opened again,
lay together until we bade farewell. I'd found peace,
Mother, in which I could start to grieve for you.

She's on a rickety step-ladder, crowbar
wrenching old nails out of logs.
I've flown away, left her to say goodbye
to the cabin we'd transformed into a home
— ten weeks to close the eyes
of three years of love and hate and play.

The well we drilled. Five hundred feet
through granite, until water gushed
at 58 degrees, whatever season.
Bathroom we constructed. No need now
to hike through snow, squat above a hand-dug hole,
wind off the Divide whipping round bare thighs.
Garden created out of virgin mountainside
— riddling scanty soil, extracting mica shards,
foraging for rocks to fashion walls
we'd view in all lights at every angle
dismantling them, rebuilding
until they shaped the spirit of the place.

Grime-cloaked, function long forgotten,
nails creak with fury as she wrests them out.

Hot-tub it took six drunk men to carry up the hill,
in which we'd float as shooting stars exploded
snowflakes spiralled down
lodged in our hair, or hissing, drowned.
Bay-window cantilevered above a precipice,
we'd loll at dawn with bitter coffee,
dog outstretched between us, one eye closed
— or at sundown, feet caressing
watch eagles glide the valley
lightning rampage the peaks
yellow rectangles flick on below us.

The final nail clinks to the floor.
She listens as the logs breathe out.

They met only in my head: Mallory, famed mountaineer,
Everest his great white whale, which possibly
he conquered the day it swallowed him;
and you, whole life in one small village,
Frodsham Hill, 500 feet, your highest peak.

Mallory, who reclining above Llanberis cliffs,
with friends and brandy, after a cool day climbing,
fumbled in his pockets, failed to find his pipe
remembered laying it on a ledge, half-way up,
his lunchtime smoke — stumbled off into the dusk
came back in half-an-hour or so, lit up.
Next morning they graded his route: impossible.

Today, wandering your house, into the room
used only when Aunt Doris came to tea,
prodding at a blister in the yellow architrave,
an old tale surfaces. I'm here, asleep,
in my wicker cot that if I close my eyes
still smells of straw, the window-light becoming
— when a wind-gust slams the door
as you chat across the washing-lines with Mrs Job —
the only route to reach your child.

But it's tiny, high above the ground,
the outside ledge two inches wide at most.
Yet, flattened to the glass, on tiptoes,
you curled fingers round the frame,
hauled yourself up and through — me still oblivious.

I grade it now: impossible. Too narrow for an adult,
you could have wriggled in only by peristalsis.

I close my eyes. The house begins to shimmer.
I will you to come back, rescue me again. And yes
you're smiling through a tent of auburn hair
as you breast-stroke down to me, shins bleeding.

Threads more tangled than we'd thought
we're back together, on probation,
kid-gloved, bruises fading.

We pad barefoot through snow
with coffee-pot, two mugs, slide
into the hot-tub's lacerating heat,
sip and watch the dawn-sky range
through every shade of scarlet.
Steam rises, freezes in our hair,
sunlight slinks the valley,
the town begins to clear its throat.

You're sitting stiffly
I offer a massage, you straddle me,
your head rests on my shoulder
while my fingers do the talking
I drink the fragrance of your hair.
Dream-haze until I'm quickened
by a tremor of your thighs,
my mouth dries at a new vision,
lovemaking in our tub, here, now.

As I stroke your forehead,
whisper it to you, your eyes
have trouble holding mine,
I feel impelled to ask,
ignore your change of tack
and ask again. Your eyes
drift back to me, apologise.

His sweat-smell wafts from clouding water,
threads of semen snake our thighs,
I slip, swallow, spit out a curly hair
whose shade of brown I do not recognise.

If I kneel, palm her stomach
where that white scar is
I feel faint warmth,
but my mirror doesn't mist
however long I hold it
to her mouth. Each week
she sinks and spreads
and leaks away, mingles
with shapeless ones below.

She's in the pit, topmost
of my tangled pile of lovers
whom time and pressure
have pureed lower down.
When I try to raise her
she dissolves. Her smile
is twisted sideways,
she tastes of sediment,
her nipple sucks my fingertip.

***

Angry with you? The wise man's wrong. Not you, Mother,
who lifted me from nightmare
drew me in until my breathing slowed to yours.

Not your fault you had to sheath yourself in glass
to face the world.
Only natural I did so, too.

Curved, thick glass, distorting everything I see,
I can't break out to touch
and no-one can break in — not even you.

One-way glass on which I watch you battering,
eyes swollen. Your knuckles start to bleed.
Yes, the wise man's right. I'm glad you're hurting.

Once more on the doorstep. I've left the key inside.
One tug on the rapper, muffled echo from the house
and I'd be off, walking swiftly, not looking round,
past the corrugated fence painted green each year
trapping millions of flies we'd try to rescue
with your tweezers, amputating legs and wings,
but not the desperate buzz, breaking to a sprint
past the long-demolished warehouse, lilac house,
bootmenders, track to Fletcher's field,
bursting round the corner into Vicarage Lane,
out of your sight, the suction of your waving.

Yet I still can't close the door. Why,
you're not here any more, Geoff's paint
has expunged you as surely as those flies?

Not you I'm afraid to say farewell to but myself,
that part of me your TCP would always cure.

So deeply abandoned, how could you find courage
to let go? Not your fault I was the same,
preserving dreams, eternal thoughts in my old ledger,
spiders in blobs of candle-wax; hating Geoff
when you put him in the cot I'd always known,
me into a sterile bed.

Not your fault either that when her spirit
wandered off to other glades
I wound arms and legs around her,
hung on, however hard she clawed.

Did you ever learn to hate? I found it easy.
Yet the most violent thing I heard you say
was "Your Aunt Lil is a fidget."

Not your fault, I keep saying. But those words
come only from my head.

All those silver stars for being good. Better
if you'd missed a few, shown me it was OK to be bad.
If so I might have reined myself instead of going wild,
sympathised when she went off the rails. Not enough
to ply your children with love and apple pie.
But you couldn't have done more. Don't cry.

Each time they hear your name, your grandkids smile
as if you were a younger sister in their care;
except Meg, who scowls, pulls her wellies on, stomps off.

I no longer care if your death-mask was more honest
than the eighty years that came before. If it wasn't
we were right to love you. If it was
and you harboured your fury at the world
we should love you even more.

Last warm day of autumn. We amble up the hill,
shuffle through chestnut shells, crisp leaves,
spread the table-cloth on springy grass.
You've baked a ham, sliced thick, a crusty loaf
with cold pie, buttered scones. She's brought violets.

As we eat, her questions prompt you to paint pictures
of your youth. You show her photos I've not seen
in the locket round your neck; one of the rock
by which you saw the badger
the night he proposed to you, sixty years ago.

Afterwards, you doze, she sucks green smoke,
wanders off into the oaks. She won't come back.

I fold the cloth into a pillow for you,
lay the violets in your hand, stroll down Silver Pin
past the Snake Tree where we once hanged Ernest Moon,
skirt a ring of sleeping cows in Mr Maddock's field,
close the door to your house in Lupin Lane.